Why Mammals Have Fur

WHY MAMMALS HAVE FUR

DOROTHY HINSHAW PATENT

PHOTOGRAPHS BY
WILLIAM MUÑOZ

COBBLEHILL BOOKS/DUTTON
NEW YORK

For Lex, Lisa, and Alex

ACKNOWLEDGMENTS

The author and photographer wish to thank the following for their help with this book: Año Nuevo State Reserve, California; Arizona Sonora Desert Museum; Brookfield Zoo; Cincinnati Zoo; Doug Allard's Trading Post; Fossil Rim Wildlife Park; Henry Doorly Zoo; Knoxville Zoo; Lincoln Park Zoo; Lowry Park Zoo; Marine World Africa U.S.A.; Minnesota Zoo; National Bison Range; Northwest Trek; Roland Smith; St. Louis Zoo; and Wolf Scat Ranch.

Library of Congress Cataloging-in-Publication Data

Patent, Dorothy Hinshaw.
    Why mammals have fur / Dorothy Hinshaw Patent ; photographs by
William Muñoz.
    p. cm.
    Includes index.
    ISBN 0-525-65141-1
    1. Mammals—Juvenile literature. 2. Fur—Juvenile literature.
    3. Hair—Juvenile literature. [1. Mammals. 2. Fur. 3. Hair.]
    I. Muñoz, William, ill. II. Title.
    QL706.2.P39 1995
    599'.047—dc20 94-28064 CIP AC

Published in the United States by Cobblehill Books,
an affiliate of Dutton Children's Books,
a division of Penguin USA Inc.,
375 Hudson Street, New York, New York 10014
Designed by Charlotte Staub
Printed in Hong Kong   First Edition
10 9 8 7 6 5 4 3 2 1

Contents

Zebra foals may learn to recognize the stripe patterns of their mothers.

1.
ANIMALS WITH FUR

Fuzzy, furry, soft, and cuddly—everyone likes animals with fur. We happily stroke our cats and pet our dogs, and we are dazzled by the striking color patterns in the coats of animals like tigers, giraffes, and zebras. But have you ever wondered why animals have fur? What does it do for them?

Fur is one of the key traits that makes mammals such successful animals. Mammals are found almost everywhere— bats that fly in the air, otters that swim in the water, moles that burrow in the earth.

One reason mammals can live in so many places is their furry coverings. Mammals are warm-blooded animals. That means their body temperatures stay just about constant, no matter how cold or warm their surroundings are. It takes a lot of energy to maintain that warmth. The built-in fur coats of most mammals help hold in their body warmth, just as feathers do for birds. Without a protective outer coating, warm-blooded animals wouldn't survive. They wouldn't be able to find enough food to fuel their internal heaters. As it is, mammals need to eat about ten times as much as cold-blooded animals of the same size.

Fur protects animals like this polar bear from the wind.

Claws, as well as fur, are made from keratin.

What Is Fur?

No one is sure how fur originated. Reptiles have protective scales that cover their bodies, and the feathers of birds seem to have evolved from those scales millions of years ago. But fur grows in a quite different way from either scales or feathers. Scientists think hair evolved from tiny sensory bumps that grew between the scales and helped ancient reptiles sense their environment. Some mammals today have scales on parts of their bodies, like those on a rat's tail or an armadillo's shell. Hairs grow between these scales, evidence that the scientists may be right.

Each individual hair grows from a tiny pocket in the skin, called a *follicle*. A bump called a *papilla*, at the base of the follicle, produces cells that die and become compressed to make the hair.

These cells are packed with a tough material called *keratin*. In addition to keratin, hairs may also contain coloring material and tiny air pockets.

The center of the hair is called the *medulla*, made up of dead cells and air spaces. Around the medulla is the *cortex*. The cortex is quite dense and contains the pigment, or coloring material. The outside covering of the hair, called the *cuticle*, is actually a layer of tiny, microscopic scales. The scale pattern of different kinds of animal differs. Experts can tell what kind of animal a hair comes from by studying its scale pattern.

Kinds of Hair?

The fur coat of most animals is made up of two kinds of hair. The outer coat consists of guard hairs, which are long and straight. Underneath the guard hairs of most mammals is a dense layer of soft, fine underfur. The underfur hairs are somewhat flattened,

You can see the long guard hairs in the coat of this African buffalo. Also notice the thick fur protecting the big ears.

Bison hair. The darker, finer fur underneath is the underfur, topped by some strands of guard hairs.

which makes them wavy. There are usually about a dozen underfur hairs for each guard hair. It is the underfur that traps air in pockets that help insulate the body, holding in warmth.

Mammals also have some specialized hairs. Eyelashes are thick hairs that protect the eyes. Whiskers are especially important modified hairs on the faces of most mammals. Whiskers are long and thick. Inside the follicle of a whisker are many nerve endings. When a whisker brushes against an object, its movement stimulates the nerve cells, which send messages to the brain about the environment. Whiskers are very sensitive. A blindfolded cat can find its way around and even catch mice by using its whiskers to tell exactly where things are.

The quills of porcupines are actually giant hairs. They are thick but hollow. The tip of a quill is very sharp. It has tiny barbs that point backward like the top of an arrow, so the quill is hard to remove.

Rhinoceroses have horns that are made up of countless compressed hairs. The rhinoceros horn is a very powerful weapon that can penetrate metal.

Cats have very sensitive whiskers.

Porcupines are well protected by their quills.

The rhinoceros's horn is made up of compressed hair.

The thick, soft fur of a sea otter holds air bubbles when the animal is underwater, insulating it from the cold. *Roland Smith*

2.
LIVING
WITH FUR

$\mathbf{F}$ur may be part of what makes mammals as successful as they are. But fur can have its drawbacks as well as its advantages.

Living in the Water

Fur is excellent at keeping animals warm in the air. But when most fur gets wet, it no longer holds air bubbles and thus loses its insulating ability. Sea otters deal with this problem in a unique way. They have the most dense fur of any animal, with up to a million hairs per square inch all over their bodies! Their soft thick fur is able to trap air bubbles that insulate their bodies when they dive for food. Sea otters spend a fair amount of time on land, where their fur also protects them from the cold air.

Marine mammals such as whales and dolphins, which never leave the water, have no fur at all, expect a few hairs they lose before they are even born. Instead, a layer of thick fat, called *blubber*, beneath the skin insulates them from the cold. Their skin is smooth, so their bodies slide easily through the water. Some whales do have a few bristles around the mouth.

The sleek body of the killer whale is insulated by a layer of blubber under the skin instead of with hair.

Seals, sea lions, and walruses spend time both in and out of the water. They have thick blubber and dense coats of short fur. The fur helps protect them when they are out of the water resting or during the breeding season, while the blubber insulates them in the water.

Animals with Little Fur

The largest land mammals, such as elephants, rhinoceroses, and hippopotamuses, hardly have any fur. They live in warm climates, and their bodies are warm enough to hold in heat.

Elephants have only a few scattered strands of hair.

A few other mammals have little or no fur. Naked mole rats, which spend their entire lives underground, have very sparse fur. Their body temperature is lower than that of most mammals, and their burrows stay within a very narrow temperature range around that of the animals' bodies. Thus, the naked mole rats do not need fur coats to keep their bodies warm.

The closest relatives to humans—chimpanzees and other apes—have plenty of hair. But humans do not have enough hair to keep their bodies warm in cool climates. Scientists have many ideas as to why humans lost most of their hair over time, but we can never be sure how it happened. Wherever we live, we can wear the right amount of clothing to make up for our lack of hair. Perhaps human ancestors began losing furry coats when they learned how to make and wear clothes.

Too Much of a Good Thing

Fur does such a good job that it can cause problems in warm climates, even to animals that are not especially large. For this

This Bactrian camel is shedding its thick winter coat.

Wolves have beautiful thick coats in winter.

Reindeer (domesticated caribou) fur

reason, animals that live where summers are warm and winters are cold change coats along with the season. This change in fur is called molting, or shedding. The old fur falls off as new fur grows to replace it.

The summer and winter coats of animals can be very different. A winter wolf looks beautiful with its thick luxurious coat, while a wolf in summer may appear awkward and scrawny to the human eye. Some animals change the color of their coats to match the season. Deer in summer have brownish coats, while their winter fur is more gray, which blends in with winter's muted colors. A number of animals, such as snowshoe hares, short-tailed weasels, and arctic foxes, grow gleaming white winter coats that help disguise them against the snow and ice.

Where the climate is especially harsh, fur can protect its wearer with a special trait. Hairs in the coats of caribou, polar bears, and some other northern animals are hollow, providing an extra layer of insulating air. Scientists have discovered that polar bear hairs serve as miniature solar heaters. They funnel the energy of the sun's ultraviolet rays directly to the animal's black skin, warming the body. The hollow hairs also give the polar bear more buoyancy in water, helping it stay afloat when it swims.

Polar bear fur

In summer, Arctic foxes are gray, with white markings.

In winter, Arctic foxes turn snowy white. *Kevin Burke, Jr.*

11

The caracal has long tufts of fur on the tips of its ears.

3.
THEIR BEAUTIFUL FUR

Fur comes in almost every color, from pure white to glossy black, and its length varies greatly. The colors of fur serve a variety of functions, from camouflage to showing off. Hair length may serve practical purposes, like maintaining body temperature. But it can also set off features that are important for social interactions. Scientists haven't always figured out the function of special colors or tufts of hair sported by animals.

Making Color

How are all the colors of mammals produced? Surprisingly, only a few chemicals are involved. White fur actually has no coloring at all—the whiteness is caused by the scattering of light of all colors by tiny air spaces in the hair. Black, on the other hand, is brought about by a pigment, or colored substance, called *melanin* found in droplets in the hair.

Different forms of melanin are responsible for most fur colors. A lot of one sort of melanin in droplets of one shape produces black. A small amount in differently shaped droplets

Colobus monkeys are black and white.

13

The golden lion tamarin is a
beautiful reddish-gold color.

will make the hair tan colored. A chemically different form of
melanin produces reddish or yellowish hairs, depending on its
amount.

Warning Colors

Animals with special ways to protect themselves often sport
bright colors that warn possible predators to stay away. The
bright colors of poison arrow frogs and of bitter-tasting monarch
butterflies are good examples. Few mammals have warning
colors, however. Skunks, with their black-and-white markings,
are obvious night and day. If another animal gets too close, a
skunk will raise its magnificent striped tail in warning. Any
creature that ignores the warning risks getting sprayed with the
skunk's stinging, stinking spray.

Some kinds of porcupines have black-and-white striped
quills. When threatened, the porcupine turns its dangerous tail
and back toward the threat and rattles its quills noisily.

Camouflage

Many animals seem to melt into their surroundings. Unless it moves, a deer in the woods or a mouse in the grass is just about invisible. Such animals blend in for more than one reason. The most obvious color of a deer's coat is gray or brown, which matches its surroundings. But if you look closely, you will notice that the animal's belly is light in color. This type of coloration, where the top is darker than the bottom, is called *countershading*. The light from the sky illuminates the top of the animal and shadows the lower parts. If the animal were uniform in color, the top part in the light would look lighter in color than the bottom part in the shade, making the animal stand out from the background. Countershading makes up for this difference in lighting. The part in the light is darker, while the shadowed areas are lighter. The result is a uniform color that blends in with the surroundings.

Both prey animals and predators, like this cougar, may show countershading. Notice the lighter color of its chest, which is likely to be in shadow.

15

Notice the more closely spaced spots on the back of the cheetah, compared to those on its lower sides.

This sloth in the zoo doesn't have algae growing on its fur, but its brown coat and coarse fur blend in perfectly with the branches.

Animals with patterns can show a variation of countershading. A cheetah has more closely spaced spots on its back than its belly, and a zebra's stripes are wider above than below. These differences help the animals melt in with the grasses of the African savannah where they live.

Sloths, which live in tropical forests, can turn green from algae growing on their brown fur. The green color helps these sluggish creatures blend in perfectly with their surroundings, making them almost impossible to see.

Patterns That Confuse

Color patterns like those of cheetahs and zebras are called *disruptive coloration.* They help break up the outline of the animal, making it difficult to see where it begins and ends. They also help it blend in with tall grasses and brush.

The stripes of zebras may serve another function. Each individual animal has its own unique striping pattern. Some scientists think this helps the zebras recognize one another, especially helping a foal pick its mother out in the crowd.

Color patterns in the fur can send other messages. Some big cats have dark bands of color or spots on the backs of their ears. The prey animals can't see them, but cubs can keep track of their mothers by focusing on the marks on their ears.

When a predator goes after prey, knowing which end of a potential meal is the head and which is the tail is very useful. A bite at the tail can result in nothing more than a mouthful of fur. But a strike at the neck can be deadly. Some animals, such as short-tailed weasels in winter, have prominent markings such as contrasting tail tips that attract the eye to the tail end. Others, like raccoons, have marks that disguise the location of their eyes.

The magnificent striped tails of ring-tailed lemurs seem to serve other functions. When the animals are looking for food on the ground, they hold their tails erect, making it easy for individ-

The okapi, which lives in the dense rain forests of Africa, shows striking disruptive coloration.

A raccoon's mask disguises the location of its eyes, which can help protect it against predators.

uals to keep track of others in their group. During the mating season, male ring-tailed lemurs rub their tails against special glands on their forearms that produce a strong scent. Then they flick their tails at rivals, sending droplets of the scent in their direction. Other animals also use fur to help hold scents that carry social messages.

Young mammals are often differently colored from their parents. Scientists believe there are a number of reasons for this. The spots of a deer fawn help camouflage it as it rests along in the brush while its mother is away feeding. A cheetah cub has a coat that resembles the powerful ratel, an aggressive animal than can take care of itself. This resemblance may help protect young cheetahs from predators like leopards. Most often, the different color of the young makes it easier for others of their kind to recognize them as youngsters.

A newborn bison is cinnamon in color, while its mother is brown.

Long Hair, Short Hair

Fur itself, however it is colored, can transmit information about an animal's intentions. Each guard hair has muscles that can contract to make the hair stand erect. When the weather is cold, an animal may fluff up its coat to increase its insulating ability. But fluffing up can also make an animal look bigger and therefore more threatening. When a cat is ready to defend itself, it raises and arches its tail with the fur standing out, and it fluffs out its body

This striped hyena looks sleek. But when it threatens another animal, it can raise its long hackles, making it look much bigger than it is.

This young baboon hangs onto its mother's fur.

fur. An aggressive dog raises the fur along its back, called its *hackles*, especially along its shoulders.

Long hair comes in handy for animals that carry their babies with them. Young opossums, monkeys, apes, and other animals grab onto their mothers' fur when they take rides.

Fur can also protect animals in special places. The foreheads of bison bulls sport thick, curly hair that helps cushion the blows of fights during the mating season. Desert mammals may have fine hairs that protect their ears from getting sand into them.

One of the most practical uses for hair is getting rid of flies. Many animals have a tuft of fur at the end of the tail for swishing away flies and other pesky insects. The horse's especially long tail is perhaps nature's best flyswatter.

The sand cat has a dense layer of hairs that protect its ears from the sand.

During the nineteenth century, the beaver was trapped mercilessly for its luxurious fur.

4.
PEOPLE AND FUR

For thousands of years, people in northern regions relied on animal fur to keep them warm. They had no centrally heated buildings and woven fabrics to keep them warm, only what they could get from nature. Animal hides also provided clothing for people in warmer climates. The fur-cloaked hides of some animals were considered more valuable than others, and the hides of certain species might be reserved for tribal chiefs. Furs sometimes had special signficance in religious ceremonies and in dances.

Fur Traders

During the eighteenth and nineteenth centuries, fur trappers and traders from Europe descended on North America, where valuable fur-bearing animals like sea otters and seals lived along the coasts and beaver, mink, and otter could be found inland. Many of these invaders were cruel and greedy. They slaughtered native people who got in their way as well as countless animals. The result was death and near slavery for many native tribes and the

Elephant seals have a short, dense fur coat.

23

near extinction of many animal species. Much of the exploration of the American West was stimulated by the possibilities for the fur trade. The main goal of the famous Lewis and Clark expedition was the search for fur trapping and trading opportunities.

Because of the intensive killing, sea otters became so rare by the early 1900s that people feared they would disappear completely. Northern elephant seals, once common from just north of San Francisco Bay all the way to islands off the coast of Mexico, were thought to be extinct in 1884. A few years later, a few animals were discovered on one Mexican island. With government protection, the northern elephant seal has now almost repopulated its whole range. Some fur-bearing species have never recovered from the effects of the fur trade and are still endangered.

Fur-wearing Today

Nowadays, we have plenty of ways to keep warm without wearing animal furs. We even have fake fur fabrics that bear attractive spots like the leopard or rich colors like the mink. Many people believe that no one should wear furs anymore. Wild animals that are trapped to provide furs are usually caught in leg-hold traps than can cause great pain. Animals on fur farms that are raised for fur are generally kept in cages, without the freedom to roam and to experience the normal life of a wild animal.

Wolf fur makes the best trimming for parka hoods that keep people's faces warm in the bitter Arctic cold.

In the extreme cold of the far north, however, fur can still be the best way to be protected against the bitter weather. Parkas are often trimmed with wolf fur, for example, because it doesn't become encrusted by ice from the breath of the person wearing the parka. Reindeer are a domesticated European version of the caribou. The Lapp people of northern Europe raise reindeer for their meat and hides. Because reindeer hides have hollow hairs, they are lightweight and especially well-insulated. The underside of the hide can be coated with a waterproof material. Then it can be used under a sleeping bag, keeping the sleeper warm even on the ice.

For generations, Native Americans have used porcupine quills for decorations on their clothing. Today, the quills are popular in jewelry making. Since the quills can be gotten from porcupines hit by cars, the animals don't have to be killed solely to obtain the quills.

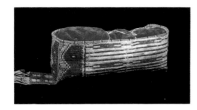

Porcupine quills have been used by Native Americans for generations, as on this Sioux cradleboard made during the 1870s.

The Special Fur Called Wool

Sheep are domesticated animals that do not shed their coats like their wild ancestors. Instead, their fine hair keeps growing and keeps them warm in the winter. With the arrival of spring, the sheep are shorn of their dense wool. The wool is cleaned, spun into yarn, and made into blankets, sweaters, and other articles of clothing.

Nature gave mammals fur, which serves them in so many important ways. We can appreciate the beauty of animals' coats, and we can enjoy stroking the soft fur of our pets. We can also continue to enjoy the special kind of warmth that natural fibers bring, thanks to sheep and their special kind of woolly fur.

Sheep wool

Sheep are domesticated mammals raised for their wool.

25

INDEX